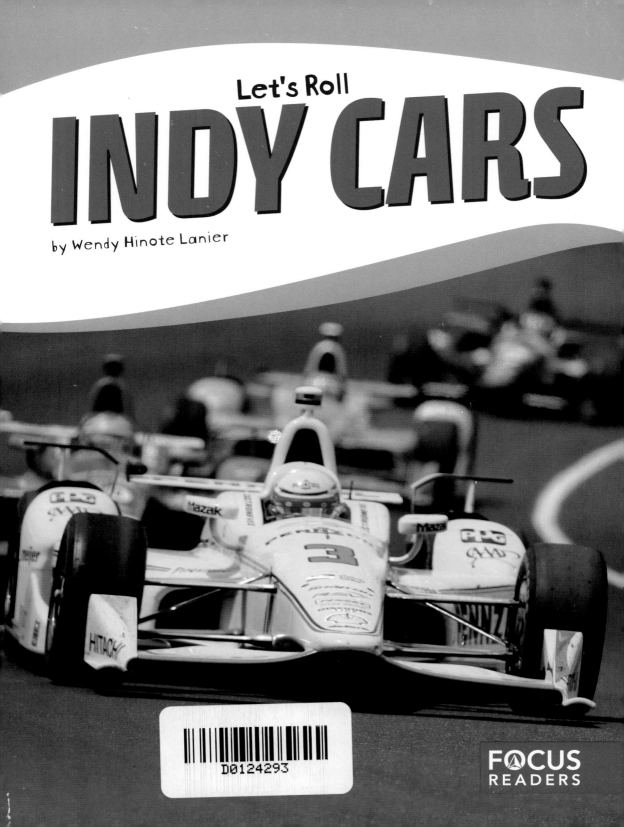

Let's Roll

INDY CARS

by Wendy Hinote Lanier

FOCUS
READERS

www.northstareditions.com

Produced for North Star Editions by Red Line Editorial.

Photographs ©: Jeff Roberson/AP Images, cover, 1; Michael Allio/Icon Sportswire/ AP Images, 4–5; Action Sports Photography/Shutterstock Images, 7, 25; HodagMedia/iStockphoto, 9, 22–23, 29; AP Images, 10–11, 13; HodagMedia/ Shutterstock Images, 15, 16–17, 26–27; Sergei Bachlakov/Shutterstock Images, 19; Zoran Karapancev/Shutterstock Images, 21

ISBN
978-1-63517-051-1 (hardcover)
978-1-63517-107-5 (paperback)
978-1-63517-208-9 (ebook pdf)
978-1-63517-158-7 (hosted ebook)

Library of Congress Control Number: 2016951024

Printed in the United States of America
Mankato, MN
November, 2016

About the Author

Wendy Hinote Lanier is a native Texan and former elementary teacher who writes and speaks to children and adults on a variety of topics. She is the author of more than 20 books for children and young people. Some of her favorite people are dogs.

TABLE OF CONTENTS

3	28
4	29
5	26
6	12
7	7
8	22
9	3
10	77
11	98
12	14
13	9
14	27
15	6
16	42
17	2
18	10
19	11
20	20
21	19
22	8
23	24
24	18
25	63
26	15
27	61
28	88
29	16
30	25
31	41
32	4
33	35

CHAPTER 1

THE INDIANAPOLIS 500

It's race day at Indianapolis Motor Speedway. The Indianapolis 500 is about to start. Thirty-three engines roar to life. The noise they make seems to shake the ground.

 Indianapolis Motor Speedway is one of the most famous race tracks in the United States.

In the stands, nearly 400,000 spectators cheer wildly. For a moment, the crowd is louder than the engines.

The person who starts the race waves a green flag. The 500-mile

THE BRICKYARD

The Indianapolis Motor Speedway is often called the Brickyard. That's because the track was originally covered in bricks. Little by little, the bricks were covered with **asphalt**. By 1961, the entire track was asphalt except for a 36-inch (91-cm) strip.

▷ **Indianapolis Motor Speedway's famous strip of bricks marks the finish line.**

(805-km) race is under way. The cars head into the first turn on the oval-shaped track. Forty seconds later, they have completed the first of 200 laps.

For the next three hours, drivers compete for the lead. Race officials keep a close watch on the position and time of each car. At last, drivers see the checkered flag. Fans roar their approval as the winner crosses the finish line.

FUN FACT

Winners of the Indy 500 are given a bottle of milk to celebrate their win.

 Drivers can have average speeds of greater than 180 miles per hour (290 km/h).

CHAPTER 2

INDY CAR HISTORY

In the early 1900s, the car business was brand new. As new models were built, carmakers started looking for ways to test them. They built a test track near the city of Indianapolis, Indiana.

In the first Indianapolis 500, mechanics rode with the drivers.

They began hosting short races on the track.

In 1911, the carmakers held a long race to attract more publicity. They wanted people to see their newest car models. They decided the race would be 500 miles (805 km) long. The Indianapolis 500 was born.

FUN FACT

Approximately 90,000 people paid $1 each to see the first Indianapolis 500 in 1911.

▷ **George Souders won the 1927 Indianapolis 500.**

By the mid-1920s, the Indianapolis 500 had become a high-paying race for professional drivers. The race cars had no tops and only one seat.

Racing mechanics **tinkered** with the engines to make them go faster. The cars became known as Indy cars because they were designed

A CONFUSING BEGINNING

The first Indy 500 was a confusing mess. There were no electronic sensors to help keep track of the cars. As the leaders began to lap the slower cars, it was difficult to tell who was winning. Finally, after 6 hours and 42 minutes of racing, Ray Harroun was declared the winner.

▷ **Today's Indy cars have top speeds of approximately 230 miles per hour (370 km/h).**

and built especially for the Indianapolis 500. Today, there is a whole series of Indy car races.

CHAPTER 3

WHAT IS AN INDY CAR?

Indy cars are built for racing. They are similar to Formula 1 cars. But Indy cars run on oval tracks. Indianapolis Motor Speedway is the most famous of the oval tracks.

 During a pit stop, one crew member refuels the car while others change the tires.

Indy cars are built according to INDYCAR rules. The engine can weigh no less than 248 pounds (112 kg). The entire car must weigh

WHO MAKES THE RULES?

Over the years, several organizations have overseen Indy car races. Today, Indy cars are built and raced according to rules set by INDYCAR. Winners of each race are awarded points. The season's top point scorer is declared the series champion and receives a $1 million bonus.

 An Indy car's engine is in the back of the car, behind the driver's seat.

at least 1,570 pounds (712 kg).

Racing teams try to keep their cars

as close to the minimum weight

as possible.

Although lightweight, Indy cars have powerful engines. The engines are tuned to produce between 500 and 700 horsepower. Indy cars are open-wheeled, single-seat cars. They have front and rear **air foils**, usually called wings. The wings

FUN FACT

Pit crews start Indy cars with an external motor. If the engine stalls during the race, the driver has no way to restart it.

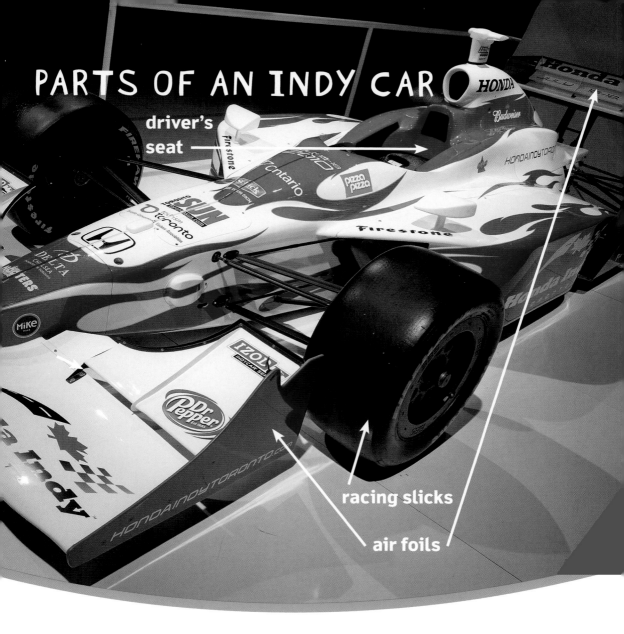

PARTS OF AN INDY CAR

driver's seat

racing slicks

air foils

create **downforce** that keeps the car on the track.

CHAPTER 4

INDY CARS OF TODAY

Today's Indy cars are built on a Dallara **chassis**. They are powered by either Honda or Chevrolet V6 turbocharged engines.

Wings and bodywork added to the chassis are called aero kits.

> All Indy cars use the same chassis.

The aero kits give the cars their **aerodynamics**. They also direct air over the oil cooler and the radiator to help cool the engine.

Fuel cells are used to prevent spillage and fires in case of a crash. A fuel cell is made of rubber. It is coated with a strong protective

An Indy car's aerodynamic shape helps it move more quickly.

covering and filled with foam. This

keeps fuel from gushing out if the

cell is broken in a crash.

THE DALLARA CHASSIS

All Indy cars use the Dallara chassis. It is built of carbon fiber with an aluminum honeycomb core. The engine is part of the chassis and holds the car together. The gearbox and rear **suspension** bolt to the back of the engine. The driver compartment, fuel cell, and front suspension bolt to the front. Side pods are also included in the chassis. They are the bodywork on the side of the car.

Dallara has been making the chassis for Indy cars since 1997.

26

FOCUS ON
INDY CARS

Write your answers on a separate piece of paper.

1. Write a sentence explaining the main ideas of Chapter 2.

2. Do you think Indy car drivers should be allowed to use a different chassis? Why or why not?

3. What creates downforce on an Indy car?
   - A. radiator
   - B. air foils
   - C. turbocharged engines

4. What might happen if Indy cars did not have fuel cells?
   - A. Crashes would be more dangerous.
   - B. The cars would not be able to go as fast.
   - C. Drivers would have to make more pit stops.

5. What does **publicity** mean in this book?

    A. money

    B. new cars

    C. attention

In 1911, the carmakers held a long race to attract more **publicity**. They wanted people to see their newest car models.

6. What does **spectators** mean in this book?

    A. loud noises that people make

    B. people who watch something

    C. the places where people sit

In the stands, nearly 400,000 **spectators** cheer wildly. For a moment, the crowd is louder than the engines.

Answer key on page 32.

GLOSSARY

aerodynamics
The ability of an object to move through the air.

air foils
Objects designed to create downward forces as air flows over the surface.

asphalt
A mixture of gravel, crushed rock, and other substances used in paving.

chassis
The frame, wheels, and machinery of a motor vehicle that supports the body.

downforce
A force produced by air resistance that pushes down on a vehicle, increasing its stability.

lap
To increase the lead over another driver by one circuit around the track.

suspension
The system that connects a car to its wheels.

tinkered
Made small changes in an effort to improve something.

TO LEARN MORE

BOOKS

Monnig, Alex. *Behind the Wheel of an Indy Car.* Mankato, MN: The Child's World, 2016.

Scheff, Matt. *Indy Cars.* Minneapolis: Abdo Publishing, 2015.

Von Finn, Denny. *Indy Cars.* Minneapolis: Bellwether Media, 2011.

NOTE TO EDUCATORS

Visit **www.focusreaders.com** to find lesson plans, activities, links, and other resources related to this title.

INDEX

A
aerodynamics, 24
aero kits, 23–24
air foils, 20

C
checkered flag, 8
Chevrolet, 23

D
Dallara chassis, 23, 26
downforce, 21

E
engines, 5–6, 14, 18, 20,
   23–24, 26

F
Formula 1, 17
fuel cells, 24, 26

H
Harroun, Ray, 14
Honda, 23

I
Indianapolis 500, 5, 8,
   12, 13, 14, 15
Indianapolis Motor
   Speedway, 5, 6, 17
INDYCAR, 18

O
oval track, 7, 17

S
suspension, 26

T
tires, 24

Answer Key: 1. Answers will vary; **2.** Answers will vary; **3.** B; **4.** A; **5.** C; **6.** B

DATE DUE

			PRINTED IN U.S.A.